PREVENTING
CHILD
SEXUAL
ASSAULT

A practical guide to talking with children

Michele Elliott

Published in association with the
Child Assault Prevention Programme
Be

Published by
BEDFORD SQUARE PRESS of the
National Council for
Voluntary Organisations
26 Bedford Square, London WC1B 3HU

ISBN 0 7199 1165 6

First published privately as *Preventing
Child Sexual Assault: A Parent's Guide to
Talking with Children* 1984

This new, enlarged edition first published
by Bedford Square Press March 1985
Reprinted April 1985
Second edition September 1985

Typeset by Vigo Press Ltd, London

Printed in Great Britain by Martin's of Berwick

CONTENTS

Acknowledgements

I gratefully acknowledge the Child Assault Prevention Project (CAP) of Women Against Rape, Columbus, Ohio, which developed many of the ideas in this book. I would also like to thank Christine Smakowska, librarian at the National Society for the Prevention of Cruelty to Children; Carolyn Okell Jones, social worker at the Tavistock Clinic; Dr Arnon Bentovim, consultant psychiatrist at Great Ormond Street Hospital for Sick Children; Patricia Crumpley, from the Tri-Valley Haven for Women; Ruth Hall, author; and Jacqueline Sallon, of the Bedford Square Press; for their kind help. I am grateful, too, to Janet Wilmoth, Daphne Joiner and my husband and sons for their support.

Child Assault Prevention Programme (CAP)

CAP was started in 1978 in Columbus, Ohio as the Child Assault Prevention Project. The local rape crisis centre, Women Against Rape, received a telephone call from a teacher. One of her students, an 8-year-old girl, had been raped and the teacher needed help in calming the fears of the child's classmates and in giving the children practical suggestions.

In response to this request, a group of concerned professionals and parents met to carry out research into sexual assault against children. The statistics convinced them that large numbers of both boys and girls were at risk. They also concluded that children needed specific information based upon reducing vulnerability to help keep them safe. From this beginning the programme has spread on a community basis throughout the United States.

The programme consists of three workshops, for parents, teachers and for children in their classrooms. The strategies are based upon common sense and realistic techniques.

For further information about CAP contact Michele Elliott, Director, Child Assault Prevention Programme, 30 Windsor Court, Moscow Road, London W2 4SN.

Introduction

This book was written to help parents, teachers and other concerned adults to protect children and to communicate with them about preventing sexual assault in a practical way using common sense.

Concern about sexual abuse of children is growing in Britain. Over the past 10 years the number of reported cases has increased considerably. It is estimated that at least 1 in 10 adults were sexually abused as children, though some studies have placed the figure much higher. While some communities have developed programmes for the victims and their families, nothing has been done in the area of prevention.

Parents are aware of the need to help their children recognize potentially dangerous situations. Yet many feel inadequate to discuss the subject properly with their offspring. Instead they supervise their children as much as possible, and rely uneasily on the good intentions of others.

This is not enough. Unfortunately, the majority (75 per cent) of assaults on children are committed by someone they know: a neighbour, friend, family member, etc. Therefore, telling children to beware only of strangers makes them more vulnerable. This is like teaching them to cross the road and to watch out for just the red cars.

What is child sexual assault?

Children are naturally affectionate and seek the attention of adults. However, when adults use children as sexual objects or partners, it is inappropriate and irresponsible behaviour. Child sexual assault is any exploitation of a child under the age of 16 for the sexual pleasure and gratification of the adult. This ranges from obscene telephone calls, indecent exposure and voyeurism such as watching a child undress to fondling, taking pornographic pictures, intercourse or attempted intercourse, rape, incest or child prostitution. It may be a single incident or events which occur over a number of years.

Who are the offenders?

Child molesters come from every class, profession, racial and religious background. Approximately 90 per cent of reported offenders are men and a large proportion are married with children. Most sex offenders lacked affection and physical contact when they were young and a high percentage were themselves abused as children. Child molesters tend to gravitate towards places, professions and activities which put them into contact with children. Although many studies are trying to establish a profile of the 'average' offender, the only current universal definition and common characteristic of child molesters is that they molest children.

Particularly disturbing are the US statistics showing that child molesters average 73 victims before they are caught. Offenders are usually able to avoid detection because they become expert at hiding their deviant behaviour from family, friends and colleagues and because children are easily coerced into silence by adult authority. A further cause for concern is that, despite the best efforts of professionals who work with child molesters, the risk of reoffending is extremely high (75 per cent). Therefore teaching children to tell and to seek help is the only effective method of prevention currently available.

The need for preventative techniques

Children must be taught how to prevent sexual assault by anyone, including adults known to the children, as well as strangers who may try to harm them. This can be done in a manner which is neither frightening nor unrealistic. It is important to talk with children because it is the lack of information which makes them vulnerable. By teaching children to avoid dangerous situations, to recognize inappropriate touching, to say no when someone tries to do something which makes them frightened or confused, to refuse to keep secrets, and to seek adult help, parents can begin to prevent sexual abuse.

It is important to realize that all children need this kind of protection. Sexual abuse of children occurs within every neighbourhood, every class and every racial background. There are also numerous recorded cases of abuse of children in care or in foster homes and of physically and mentally handicapped children. The message of prevention is the same for all children and the ideas in this book can be adapted according to the individual child, his or her level of understanding, age, cultural background or circumstances.

Adults are often concerned that talking about preventing assault will make children afraid or anxious. Yet parents teach children from the time they are very young that there are dangers in the world. Children learn not to play with matches, to avoid harmful medicines and how to cross streets. In the same way, using common sense, children can be taught to prevent sexual assault not only by strangers, but also by someone they know and trust.

Children who know preventative techniques are not only less at risk because they are informed, but they are also more confident about themselves. Parents who can talk with their children in a loving atmosphere and help them learn ways to stay safe are giving their children excellent protection.

Any adult who cares about children must recognize the problem of child sexual assault and learn to teach children about it. With our help, children can be taught to use and trust their own judgement to protect themselves and to be safe, aware and confident.

I
TEACHING CHILDREN HOW TO PREVENT SEXUAL ASSAULT

2

How to begin

There are several ways to begin a conversation with children about preventing sexual abuse. Two methods that have been used very successfully both at home and in the classroom are talking about rights and talking about good and bad touches.

Discuss the right to be safe

Explain to children that everyone has rights which should not be taken away from them. Start with simple ideas such as the right to breathe, eat, sleep, play or go to the toilet. Ask children what would happen if the right to eat was taken away from them. Would that create problems? What if they were not allowed to go to the toilet?

Children should be encouraged to think about what would happen to start them using their own judgement. Ask them to think of ways to get their rights back. One child said that if she was not allowed to eat, she would collect berries. Another said that he would go on strike and picket his house with a sign saying 'unfair to children'.

After children clearly understand this concept, use it to discuss the right to be safe. Ask them when they feel safe, and ask them to give specific examples such as 'when my parents tuck me into bed with a goodnight kiss' or 'when playing with my friends' or 'when reading a story with Mummy'. One 5-year-old said that being safe was 'not having to stay with the lions in the zoo'. Explain that sometimes people try to take away the rights of others, including the right to be safe.

Emphasize to children that they should say no and get help when someone tries to take away their right to be safe and that you will support them in this. Make sure that children understand that the right to be safe includes the right to say what happens to their own bodies. (See the following suggestions about saying no and talking with children about their bodies.)

Discuss good touches and bad touches

Another approach is to begin with an explanation of good and bad touches. You can introduce this by talking about how nice a hug or kiss can be and by asking children how they would show someone they love them (without giving a tangible gift such as a puppy or toy). One child said he would give someone he loved 1,000 hugs and kisses every day. If you have a pet, ask children what kind of touches the pet likes or dislikes. Then ask what kind of touches children like or dislike. Children may say they like soft hugs and big kisses. They often mention that tickling is fun, but not too much or too long. Many children relate that they hate being patted on the head.

Explain that children have the right to say no, even to someone they love, if they do not like a touch or a kiss. This means that children should not be forced to be affectionate with anyone, even their own parents.

Parents can help their children politely to refuse kisses or hugs that make them uncomfortable, even in an every-day situation. If necessary, explain that your child is going through a 'shy stage' or be totally honest and say that your child is learning to say no to requests that make him or her uncomfortable. If we force children to be affectionate because we as adults are embarrassed if they are not, we are not helping them. Children must begin to trust their own feelings and judgement if they are to learn to keep themselves safe.

This also means that children will have to learn that there are times when the rules of being polite do not apply and it might be necessary to break them.

There are many different cultural customs about hugging, kissing and touching. There is no reason for these to change. However, in any culture it is inappropriate for an adult to seek contact with children as a result of his or her own sexual needs or if the adult is sexually stimulated by the contact.

3

What to do next

Talk to children about their bodies

Explain to children that their bodies are their own and that no one should touch them in a way which makes them confused or uncomfortable. Teach children the correct names of the private parts of their bodies. However, if this makes you uncomfortable, another explanation is 'those parts of your body covered by your bathing suit'. By teaching children to be in control of their own bodies, we are also helping them to recognize their own feelings about good and bad touching. There is no need to frighten children with too much information. Rather, help them to become sensitive to their own feelings of comfort or discomfort.

Talk about good secrets versus bad secrets

Since offenders who are known to children often depend upon children's willingness to keep secrets, it is extremely effective to teach children, even very young ones, to say no to this request.

In some families, children are taught to keep surprises, but never to keep secrets. Another method is to teach children the difference between good and bad secrets. Ask children to suggest a good secret. They will probably mention a birthday present, or surprise party or mummy having another baby. See if they can describe a bad secret. Some examples that children have offered are: 'Daddy and Mummy getting divorced', 'knowing your friend has taken something from a shop', or 'a bully who takes away your money and you are too scared to tell'.

When children understand the difference between good and bad secrets, they are ready to be taught that no one should ask them to keep touching a secret. This applies to all touching, even if it feels good. Tell children that they should always tell a trusted adult if anyone asks them to keep such a secret.

One difficulty in dealing with child sexual assault is that sometimes the victims experience physical pleasure. This often compounds the confusion and makes the children feel that they are accomplices and that their bodies have betrayed them. By saying to children that no touches, hugs or kisses should be kept secret, you are helping them to define proper limits and giving them permission to seek adult help without feeling guilty.

Encourage children to tell

Assure your children that no matter what happens you will not be angry with them and that you want them to tell you of any incident. Explain the difference between telling tales to get someone into trouble and getting help when someone is threatening their safety. Ask children to give examples of telling tales, such as running to the teacher because another child is using the swings when they want to swing. Then talk about dangerous situations in which a child should get help. One child described a time when his bicycle had been taken from him and the teenager threatened him with a beating if he told.

Explain to children that even if they break a home or school rule which leads to them getting into difficulty, you still want to know and you will not blame them. An 11-year-old girl broke the family rule about going through the park to get home after school. A man forced her into the bushes and indecently assaulted her. He told her he would find her and kill her if she told. She eventually told her parents, who immediately comforted her and assured her that it was the offender who was guilty, not her. They did not say, 'See what happens when you don't listen?' The child knew she should not have gone across the park, but to have made her feel guilty would not have been helpful.

By giving your children the assurance that you will support them, no matter what circumstances preceded the incident, you will help them to cope better with an assault, should it occur. If you do not give this kind of assurance and mean it, your children will not tell you for fear that you will be angry with them.

Since children often feel that adults do not believe them, encourage children to keep telling until someone does and the children get help.

Bribes

Child molesters, both adults known to children and strangers, often offer children bribes in exchange for sexual favours. Children should be taught what bribes are and what those who offer bribes seek to accomplish. Explain the difference between gifts and bribes. The message that children need to learn is that gifts are given freely with no conditions and that bribes are given to make them do something they don't want to do.

Tricks

Explain to children that some people, both known adults and strangers, might try to trick them by offering them a present, money, sweets or a trip to the zoo or cinema to do something they don't like. Tell them that if that happens they should say something like, 'I must ask my mum, dad or my teacher', and get away quickly to seek help.

A common trick used by molesters is, 'Your mum is sick and asked me to take you to her.' One suggestion that many parents have used is to have a code word, known only to the parents and children. If you must send someone to collect children in an emergency, the person sent would use the agreed code.

Tell children that you want to be told if anyone offers them a bribe or tries to trick them.

Teach children to say no

Instead of teaching children to listen to and obey all adults without question, tell them that they have your permission and support to say no to protect themselves. Help them to practise saying no in an assertive way because it is very difficult for most children to say no to an adult.

In the classroom or at home, adults can help children to learn to say no by asking if it is easy to say no to someone older. Children usually say that it is difficult to refuse an adult's request or command. Explain that you are going to help them practise saying no. This will enable them to say no if someone asks them to do anything which makes them confused or uncomfortable.

Start with questions children can easily say no to such as:

Adult: 'Do you like asparagus?'

Child: 'No.'

Adult: 'Wouldn't you like an asparagus sandwich?'

Child: 'No.'

Proceed to questions requiring caution:

Adult: 'Can you tell me how to get to the cinema?'

Child: 'No.'

Most adults do not ask children for directions, so it is safer to tell children not to get involved.

Tell children that they should not enter into conversation, nor give reasons for not talking. A simple, firm 'no' is all that is required.

Proceed to trick questions such as:

Adult: 'I have some puppies in the car. Would you like to see them?'

Child: 'No.'

Children can offer suggestions and the idea of saying no in an assertive way can be learned in a safe environment. Practising will help to make saying no automatic in a potentially dangerous situation. Along with not keeping secrets and knowing about bad touching, saying no can be an especially effective deterrent against the non-violent offender who is known to the child. One man who had molested three of his four children was asked why he did not abuse the fourth. 'She said no', was his answer. However, if a child feels that he or she is in physical danger, it may be necessary to comply with the adult's demand and then seek help by telling.

Do not define people as good or bad

If children think only bad people hurt them, they will not be prepared for the person who approaches them in a manner which gains their trust. By teaching them the danger signs, you will be protecting them far better than by telling them to watch out for 'bad' people. One method of relating this is to explain that people have good and bad in them and sometimes even good people do things we do not like. Emphasise that children should say no if anyone tries to do something which makes them frightened or confused.

The mother of a 10-year-old boy said that her son had been taught to say no to strangers and was confident that he could take care of himself. One afternoon after school when the boy was alone, a man wearing a business suit and carrying a briefcase knocked on the door. The boy opened the door, using the safety chain. The man claimed that he was taking his pregnant wife to the hospital, their car had broken down and he had to telephone for an ambulance. The boy offered to telephone for him, but the man insisted that this was an emergency and there was no time to spare. The boy let him in and was sexually assaulted. His mother said that her son told her afterwards that the man had not seemed to be a 'bad person' because he was dressed 'like Daddy and did not look like a stranger'.

Children quickly take people out of the category of 'stranger'. It is important to emphasise that they should say no if anyone tries to do something which makes them frightened or confused. It is better to say no and perhaps hurt someone's feelings than to take a chance and get hurt oneself.

Answer children's questions

When children are concerned about television programmes, night-mares, newspaper reports or tragedies, answer their questions carefully and sensitively without dismissing their feelings or deny-ing the reality of the situation. This helps children to trust their own feelings and judgement and is better than telling them not to worry. Children will not share their feelings if they are not taken seriously.

However, there is no need to frighten children with too much information. Understand what children are really asking and give them the facts gradually until they are satisfied with the answer. For example, one 5-year-old girl asked her mother what rape was because she heard the word on television. The mother's response was to find out what her daughter thought it was and to proceed from there. In this case the explanation that it meant someone touching her private body parts in a way she did not like was all that was needed. If an older child had asked the same question, he or she would probably need more information and a fuller explanation. Explaining instead of avoiding is the important message so that children will feel confident in asking questions because they will know that they will receive honest answers.

Believe your children

Children do not lie about sexual assault which has occurred: they do not have the language or experience. They may, however, later deny that abuse took place to protect someone they love or because they are afraid. Children may also get the details confused because of the traumatic nature of what happened. When dealing with children, question gently but do not interrogate.

Ask for the reasons when children do not want to go to someone's house or do not like a babysitter, or when their behaviour patterns change dramatically (see page 32). Gently draw out more information about comments such as 'I don't like the way John teases me' or 'The man at the shop acts funny.' Although these comments usually indicate something harmless, parents must learn to be sensitive to what their children are trying to say. One child told her mother that her uncle teased her and she didn't like it. The mother responded that everyone gets teased growing up and she would have to get used to it. The child was very upset, but did not say anything else. Several months later, the girl was diagnosed as having gonorrhea of the throat. Her uncle called it teasing and she was too young to know better.

Create an atmosphere of trust in which children know they will be listened to and believed. They will then be encouraged to share their concerns and thus potentially harmful situations can be avoided.

Play 'what if' games

Children often ask 'what would happen if' type questions, which parents can turn into a fun learning game. Instead of answering immediately, ask your children what they think would happen. This gives them a chance to test their ideas and judgement about the world. Parents can initiate questions as well, but should be careful not to ask questions that may frighten children.

With young children it might be better to start with something like 'What would you do if a monkey came to the door?' Then, if the child is interested, ask other questions which are appropriate to his/her age. (Since the monkey is a stranger, by the way, the child should not let it in!) This can lead to a discussion of who would be let in: what if someone was dressed like Daddy or said Mummy was ill, etc. Questions like 'What if someone you know tries to touch you in a way you do not like?' should be included when the child is ready.

Playing 'what if' games, either at home or in school, is a good way for children to learn many concepts. You can start with a variety of situations not related to assaults. For example:

Adult: 'What if you saw smoke coming from your neighbour's house?'

Child: 'I would ring the fire brigade.'

Adult: 'How would you do that? Demonstrate for me.'

This would be a good way to teach a child about making 999 calls. Examples of preventative 'what if' games might be:

Adult: 'What if someone said he or she was a friend of Daddy's and asked you to go with him or her to a house?'

Child: 'I would not go and would run away if anyone got too close. I would tell a grown-up what happened.'

When the children are prepared for the more sensitive questions, ask:

Adult: 'What if a babysitter or relative you liked asked you to play secret games, and offered to let you stay up late (or give you a present or money, etc.)?'

Child: 'I would say that I am not allowed to keep secrets.'

Adult: 'What if the person insisted?'

Child: 'I would say no and say I was going to tell. Then I would tell.'

Teach children to keep safe

If children find themselves in a difficult situation, they may not be able to deal with it because they feel restrained by all the every-day rules they have been taught. In teaching children to keep themselves safe, we must tell them that there are exceptions to every rule.

For example, children are taught to be polite, not to lie, not to tell tales, and certainly not to resist adults. Yet to keep themselves safe children may need to break one or more of these rules. Parents should discuss this with their children (by using the 'what if' game) and give them permission to make exceptions.

The most important message you can teach children is that they have the right to use any method to keep themselves safe in a potentially dangerous situation. Again, using language appropriate to their age, tell children it is all right not to answer the door, to say no to someone they love, to yell, run, bite, kick, lie, break a window, etc. Remind them that the object is always to run, get away and seek adult help. Give them your permission to break all rules to protect themselves and tell them you will support them.

The father of 6-year-old Adam who was abducted and murdered said:

'Adam was a model child, he never even went to the park by himself. He never disobeyed, never. I taught him to listen to adults, to respect his elders and to be a little gentleman. I never taught him how to scream. He might be alive if he had screamed.'

More suggestions for parents

- Teach children their full names, addresses and telephone numbers.
- Do *not* teach children to answer the telephone by repeating their name or telephone number.
- Evaluate children's regular walking routes and playing places.
- Help children practise making an emergency telephone call. Write your telephone number in large print by the telephone as people often forget their own number when making a call under stress.

- Do not put names on the outside of children's clothes or books.
- Watch for negative reactions to people and explore suspicious comments children may make about adults, older children or teenagers, babysitters, etc.
- Help children to establish a network of trusted adults to whom they can turn for help.
- Teach basic techniques such as never go with a stranger, always stay two arm lengths from a stranger (demonstrate that it is difficult to grab someone from that distance), never answer the door when at home alone or admit over the telephone to being alone. Practise telephone answers such as 'My mother is in the bath. If you will leave your number, she will ring you back.'
- In the first few seconds of an attack, the child might have the advantage of surprise because the attacker is expecting a child to be passive and scared. Since getting away is the object, a child can surprise an attacker and run for help: immediate, noisy and active resistance is the key. Even very young children can be taught to yell loudly and run. An older child can be taught to yell, kick the attacker's knee with the heel of his or her foot, scrape down the attacker's inside calf in the same motion, stamp as hard as possible on the attacker's foot, and run to get away. Another technique for the older child is to bring his or her elbow into the attacker's stomach or groin and run. Remember that we are talking about a very dangerous situation in which it is possible that the child will be badly hurt and the only chance is to get away. The goal is to startle or hurt the attacker enough to run away.
- Tell children never to chase after an attacker. Tell them to leave that to the police or other adults.
- Play games involving observation skills such as looking at objects on a tray for 10 seconds and recalling them from memory. Ask a member of the family to come into the room for 10 seconds, then leave. Try to recall as many details as possible about him or her.

While travelling in the car, see who can call out registration numbers on red cars, etc.

- Check with other parents concerning your babysitter's reliability and behaviour.

- If your child has a nightmare and is afraid to go back to sleep, turn on the light and search the room with him or her. This will comfort the child far more than saying there is nothing there. It will also assure your child that you listen and believe what he or she says and that you are prepared to intervene actively to help. This kind of listening could be quite important for future communication.

- Hug and kiss your children. Most child molesters never had good hugs and kisses: in one US study 80 per cent were found to have been molested themselves as children, either physically or sexually. For children, those appropriate touches, hugs and kisses are the best gifts we can give them.

4

Helping teenagers to protect themselves

While parents want their teenagers to be independent, it is obvious that this group also needs preventative tactics to deal with common assault problems. The most frequent problem at this age is the acquaintance or date rape. Too often teenagers are afraid to hurt someone's feelings, or do not want to look foolish in front of their friends, or just do not expect someone they know to betray their trust. Therefore they may end up in a dangerous situation not knowing what to do.

Susan, age 18, was at a staff Christmas party with people from the firm she had worked with for over a year. After she had drunk too much, her 27-year-old manager insisted upon driving her home. He easily persuaded her to stop and have a cup of coffee at his flat so that her parents would not see her in such a state. Once in the flat, he threatened her, raped her seven times and left her unconscious. She woke up after he had passed out, left the flat, took a taxi home and never went back to her job. She also never told anyone or reported it to the police because, 'I went with him to the flat. The police would not believe me if I said it was rape.' Although she knows her parents would believe her, she is afraid that her father would kill the man and that her parents would worry about her every time she went out. Susan is still angry, hurt, confused and frightened by the incident.

What you should discuss
Setting limits

By deciding what needs and limits they have, teenagers will be in a better position to determine if they are getting into a situation beyond their control. These limits will change depending upon the person they are with and depending upon the teenager's age and maturity. By thinking about their own boundaries, teenagers will begin to test and trust their judgement, an important tool in keeping safe.

Setting limits can include deciding what to do if asked by friends or acquaintances to go along with something teenagers like or do not really like or feel comfortable about. What if a group of friends want to go to the cinema, have a party, go to a pub, get drunk, shoplift, try drugs, go to a disco, go somewhere for a 'kiss and a cuddle', or find some girls or boys 'ready for action'? Teenagers should think about what they want before the opportunities are presented to them.

Communicating these limits

Teenagers need to be told to communicate their limits to others: boyfriends, friends or acquaintances. Although peer group pressure is great at this age, planning in advance makes saying no easier. For younger teenagers, using parents as an excuse sometimes helps: 'My mum won't let me. . .' Parents should not be misled by their teenager's rebellious poses; many teenagers are secretly grateful to place the 'blame' on their parents.

Trusting intuition

Often teenagers do not trust their own feelings and judgement. Though they may sense they are getting into a difficult situation, they have not thought out what to do or do not want to appear silly in front of friends, so they go along until it is too late. By learning to trust that inner feeling, teenagers can avoid many potential problems.

Mike was talked into having a party while his parents were away for the evening. His friends said that they would help clean up and that his parents would 'never know'. Though he felt uncomfortable, Mike agreed because he wanted to be part of the group. Everything went well until a neighbourhood group of troublemakers gatecrashed. Mike knew immediately he should get help, but thought that by handling the situation himself he could avoid getting into difficulty with his parents.

The troublemakers began to beat the boys, molest some of the girls and wreck the house. Only then did one of the boys telephone the police, ignoring the protesting host who said that his parents would 'kill him' for allowing the party to take place. Had Mike trusted his judgement and refused to have the party, none of this would have happened.

Being aware of the behaviour of others

If someone is acting in an inappropriate way, it is best to keep a safe distance. For example, if a person in the group is making inappropriate jokes or comments, or drinking too much, or not listening and offending others, then tell teenagers not to get involved. If another person acts in an over familiar way, gets too close in a way which makes them uncomfortable, or begins touching them, teenagers should be told to say no forcefully and get help, if necessary.

Saying no and meaning it

One of the most commonly held myths is that when a girl says no, she means yes (see true/false questionnaire on page 48). To avoid any misunderstanding, girls should be told to look the person in the eye and say no in a loud, firm voice. They should make sure their body language conveys the same message. Teenage girls should remember that they have the right to say no and that kissing and cuddling should not be regarded as an open invitation to have sexual intercourse.

Becoming angry

Many people become frozen with fear and cannot think in a dangerous situation. Anger helps to focus energy and convert thoughts into action. Tell teenagers to think 'I don't deserve this' and use whatever force is necessary to get out of the difficulty. Teenagers should realize that by acting quickly and decisively, they may be saving themselves from potential harm.

Jenny had been jogging in the park, wearing her Walkman, and failed to hear the older teenage boy who approached from behind and dragged her to a secluded area. She saw people walking by, but they could not see her. She was terrified and could not remember anything from the self-defence class she was taking. However, when the boy tried to pull down her shorts, she became angry. 'I haven't done anything to him,' she thought. 'He has no right to do this to me!' With that, she yelled a deep, loud yell, pushed him hard and ran away towards the path. He was startled and ran in another direction. Jenny later remarked that her anger gave her strength she didn't know she had.

Learning self-defence

Taking a self-defence course is a good idea for those who are willing to do the necessary work and practise what they have been taught. For most teenagers or adults, knowing and practising three or four techniques would be more helpful than having so much information that it is all forgotten in a crisis. Learning how to get out of a hold, where the pressure points are on the body and how to kick, bite or hit to get away would be useful information for most people. Check what courses there are in in your local area.

Telling a trusted adult

If a teenager is raped or molested, he or she often does not tell, fearing censure by friends, humiliation or disbelief. Teenagers, too, need a network of trusted adults to whom they can turn. Parents can help teenagers work out a list or teenagers can do it on their own. They should be told to keep telling until they receive help. Adults also must learn to give help without censure. One enlightened father has told all of his children that if they ever get into a situation they cannot handle, they can telephone him and he will pick them up, no questions asked.

Knowing that the offender is responsible

This is an important message because most teenagers will not tell parents if they are attacked for fear that they will be blamed. They may also blame themselves as many victims of assault do: 'I did not follow the rules, so this is my fault.' Parents and others who deal with teenagers should emphasize that it is the offender's fault.

The facts about sexual assault

Since many people are misinformed about the realities of sexual assault, discussing facts will lead to a better understanding of the problems. If boys and girls examine the issues together so that the message is the same for both, then they can begin to understand what to expect from each other and communicate in an open and honest way.

The questionnaires on pages 41-53 can be used to introduce the subject. Teenagers should discuss the answers either with friends, parents or in the classroom.

5

How teachers can help

Teachers can help in the community effort to teach children to be safe, although they must be aware of community sensitivities and keep their classroom discussions within the guidelines that are acceptable both to parents and the school. A meeting of school and local social services personnel would be helpful in establishing these guidelines.

Teachers of all age groups will be able to adapt many of the ideas discussed earlier and use them in the classroom. Some additional ideas for specific age groups are included here for group work with children.

Pre-school children

Most nursery teachers use dolls, puppets, and stories when working with children under 5. When teaching young children about staying safe, use these tools to help the children to understand the concepts. For example, when discussing the right to be safe, use the story of Peter Rabbit. He broke the family rule about invading Mr McGregor's garden and was almost made into rabbit pie, like his father. This story will help to introduce the idea that children should tell, even if they have broken a family rule. Peter did not tell his mother about how he lost his coat because he should not have been in the garden in the first place. In addition, the concept of self-reliance can be introduced by explaining how Peter used his wits to escape from the garden.

Use dolls or puppets to portray what happens in a playground, such as one child taking away a toy from another. Ask the children what they would do, how they would help each other and how they would get adult assistance.

The dolls can be used to show good and bad touches and to dramatise the story of someone known to a child trying to do something the child disliked, such as kissing the doll when the doll obviously does not want to be kissed. Good hugs and kisses should be shown to the children.

Primary school children

Here is one method by which children in the classroom can be taught to protect themselves. Begin with a discussion of rights as mentioned earlier (see page 6). When the children clearly understand this concept, discuss the problem of bullies. Most children have had the experience of being confronted by a bully. The teacher can introduce the topic either by talking or role-playing. Here is an example:

John is playing in the park when an older, bigger boy approaches and demands John's pocket money. John gives the bully his money and is therefore unsuccessful in defending himself.

Then discuss how John felt, how the bully felt and explain that John had his right to be safe taken away. Ask the children what they would do in this situation. Be prepared for the children wanting to punch the bully on the nose and asking if that would solve the problem. 'Wouldn't the bully then hit back?' Ask the children about telling an adult and if that would mean they were telling tales, as discussed in the first part of this book. If none of the children mentions taking a friend along, suggest that having a friend, brother or sister helping to say no makes people feel stronger.

The three tactics that the children should have learned are:
- to refuse to give in to the bully
- to ask a friend or sibling to help
- to tell an adult what happened

Re-do the role-play or discuss how the child can be successful in saying no to the bully. Obviously, this must be done according to the age of the children.

If the question of the bully having a weapon is raised, explain it is far better to give the bully the money, but that they should definitely tell an adult what happened.

By relating the problem of bullies to illustrate the concept of personal safety, the teacher has made the idea of the right to be safe clear to the children. The suggestions listed earlier (see pages 6-16), such as saying no, can be introduced into later talks by referring to the bully story and asking children if they have the right to say no. These techniques help children to begin using common sense and thinking about what they might do in a variety of situations to keep themselves safe. Role-playing also can be used to portray strangers and known adults in situations with children.

Young teenagers

Having begun the lesson by talking about rights, give the questionnaire on pages 41-42 to the class. Do not collect the papers; discuss the answers which will take at least half an hour. Continue by either telling or eliciting stories of bullies and strangers, and encourage the children to talk about how they would cope in various situations. What to do if approached by a known adult can be introduced when the children are ready. One way this can be done is by using a story about a girl (or boy) who has been babysitting for an aunt and uncle. When the uncle takes the babysitter home, he tries to kiss her and she rebuffs him. The uncle then tells her that the incident must be kept a secret. Discussion should focus on the issues of secrecy and who to tell.

Older teenagers

Use the questionnaire on pages 46-47 and discuss the answers. Do not collect the papers. Relate the story on page 19 about Susan and ask the class who was at fault. This can lead to further discussion about responsibility and guilt, trusting feelings, setting limits and the other topics mentioned in chapter 4, 'Helping teenagers to protect themselves'. The teacher may wish to give lessons in basic self-defence.

Reporting cases of suspected sexual assault

Anyone who works with children should also be aware of the danger signs and who to contact for help. Although there are no national guidelines for reporting suspected child sexual abuse, concerned adults are advised to contact their local social services for suggestions on the appropriate action to take. The help organisations listed in this book on pages 37-38 are also available to give advice. The danger signs listed on page 32 provide teachers with identifiable physical and emotional characteristics they should pay attention to when they suspect child abuse.

Some children will already have been sexually abused, but have not yet told. It is important, therefore, in discussing these issues with children to make sure thay are not made to feel guilty. In one classroom workshop, an 11-year-old girl started crying and later disclosed that she had been sexually assaulted by an older cousin two years previously. She felt guilty for having kept the secret and for not having said no.

When talking with children, say that sometimes children may be placed in a situation in which they cannot say no or get help. Emphasise that this is not their fault, and that children who have survived abuse and not told are very brave, but nevertheless they should try to get help from an adult. If a child reveals having been sexually abused, use the suggestions listed on pages 35 and 36 to help deal with the disclosure. Promise to do everything in your power to protect the child, but do not promise that what is said will be kept secret. It may be necessary to approach some of the organisations listed on pages 37-38.

More suggestions for teachers

In working in the classroom, the following is a brief list of ideas which have been used successfully and which can be adapted according to community needs:

- Use the suggestions in this book to talk with children in the classroom about their right to be safe.
- Discuss the difference between telling tales to get someone into trouble and getting help when a child needs adult assistance.
- Teach children that they have a right to say no to anyone (stranger, friend, family member) who asks them to do anything which makes them feel confused, frightened or uncomfortable. Practise saying no using games.
- Talk about the difference between good secrets and bad secrets.
- Play classroom 'what if' games using a variety of situations (see page 14).
- Arrange a parents' evening to discuss how to keep children safe.
- Play games involving observation skills, such as looking at objects on a tray (see 'More suggestions for parents', page 17).
- Help children to establish a network of trusted adults by having a discussion about 'who you would tell if you had a problem?' Ask them to write a private list.
- Discuss the difference between bribes and gifts.
- Assure your children that you are available to talk with them privately, should they wish to discuss any problems.
- When a child does talk with you, give no assurance that you will keep secrets. Say you will try to help the child in any way possible,

but that you might have to talk with someone else to get help for the child.

- Encourage the children to support one another.
- Ask children to write a story or draw a picture about feeling safe or scared.
- Ask teenagers to answer the true/false questionnaires in this book (see page 41). Do not collect their papers, but have a discussion about the answers.
- Develop a project on personal safety to include topics such as road and water safety, as well as methods for keeping safe in other dangerous situations. Invite the local police to show their filmstrip 'Don't Go With Strangers' and use this to introduce a discussion about keeping safe in a variety of situations.
- If there is community interest, invite CAP to come into the school to talk with parents, teachers and children in their classrooms about teaching children to keep safe.
- In order to ensure that incidents of children being approached by strangers are reported and centrally monitored, it would be helpful if each school would designate one person, such as the secretary or head, to whom children or parents could report such incidents. Police and all parents should be notified if necessary.

II
DEALING WITH
CHILD SEXUAL
ASSAULT

6

How to recognize the danger signs

You can be alert to signs of possible sexual assault by being aware of the common characteristics shared by children who have been assaulted. While many of these behaviours are normal for growing children, it is important to remember that these behaviours can also be indicative of sexual assault and should therefore be investigated.

Examine changes in a child's normal every-day patterns including physical and emotional fluctuations such as a sudden drop in school performance, lack of concentration, onset of day or night wetting, sleep disturbances, fear of going to sleep or of the dark, regression to younger behaviour, tiredness, loss of appetite, being preoccupied in a world of his or her own, being isolated from friends, running away, stealing, lying, etc. Be concerned about personality changes such as sullenness, persistent irritability, listlessness, aggressiveness, sudden, uncharacteristic flirting or being overly affectionate in a sexual way inappropriate to the child's age. Notice if something seems to be bothering a child that he or she cannot share.

Investigate a child's lack of trust in a familiar adult or fear of being alone with a babysitter, friend, neighbour or relative. Examine medical problems such as urinary infections (particularly in young children), chronic ailments such as stomach or headaches, discomfort or pain in the genital area or any kind of sexually transmitted disease.

Although many of these symptoms apply to teenagers, they may also show signs of depression or psychosomatic illness, attempt suicide or self-mutilation. Be aware that a teenage pregnancy could be a result of sexual abuse. Pay close attention to drug or alcohol misuse, to truancy and running away. Recent research has shown that child sexual abuse is also one possible cause of anorexia and bulimia nervosa.

7

What to do if you suspect abuse

If you are worried that a child has been sexually assaulted and has not told anyone, one approach is to first talk with the child about hugs, kisses, good touches, secrets and telling as discussed earlier in this book. Do this gradually (over a period of days, if necessary), and without communicating your anxieties to the child. When you feel the child is ready, ask directly if someone has touched him or her in a way which the child either did not like or which hurt or was uncomfortable. The direct approach, made calmly, is important because children seldom respond to indirect questioning as they do not understand what is being asked.

If there is a specific physical indication of an assault, point to that part of the body and ask if anyone has touched the child there. Remain calm and do not press the child for information. Let the child tell at his or her own pace. (See chapter 8, 'What to do if an assault occurs'.)

One mother related that her 3-year-old daughter often had vaginal redness after visiting an older cousin's house. The mother did not want to question her daughter because she did not know how to begin and did not want to frighten the child.

After preparing both herself and her daughter to discuss the problem in a calm way, the mother found out that the cousin was sexually assaulting her child. As do most offenders, the cousin denied it when confronted by the child's parents.

Each adult must decide according to the circumstances how to proceed in the best interests of the child. In this case the child was supported and helped at home, but the parents decided not to bring in medical or professional help. They immediately broke off all contact with the cousin, but since their major concern was not to get the child involved in a possible court appearance, they did not contact the police. Another parent might try to have the offender put in prison to protect other children, and contact the police.

Although it is particularly difficult if the abuse is happening within the family, the concerned adult must seek help for the child. When the suspected offender is the child's parent, step-parent, or other close family member, the mother or another adult can use the same method for preparing to talk with the child. Because of the effects that this will have on the child and the family, it may be useful to get professional advice in advance. Several of the help organisations listed on pages 37-38 of this book will listen and make suggestions, on an anonymous basis if requested.

If the child does say that abuse has taken place, the subsequent safety and well-being of the child must be the first consideration. No child should be left alone with a suspected offender.

The long-term effects of abuse on a child's life depend upon the severity and duration of the attack and how the child is then cared for by family, friends and/or professionals. Some children, especially those blamed and rejected by their families, carry the scars for life and never form loving relationships as adults. Yet children are resilient and with proper care and support the healing will begin. Children who are supported have a much better chance of coping and eventually establishing stable relationships.

8

What to do if an assault occurs

Since most children do not want to cause pain to someone they love, the reaction of the adult will determine how much the child will tell. The following are guidelines on what to do if an assault occurs:

- Stay calm. Try not to transmit your anger, shock and embarrassment to your child. Remaining calm will help lessen the effect of the trauma. It will help your child to know you are now in control of a situation he or she could not cope with alone. If you have had a similar experience in childhood, this may be very difficult to do. When seeking professional help for yourself and your child (see below), you may want to talk privately about what happened to you in the past.

- Believe your child. Children do not lie about sexual abuse unless they deny it happened to protect someone.

- Reassure your child. Children often feel responsible for or guilty about the incident; emphasize that it is not the child's fault. Tell your child you are glad he or she told you.

- Encourage the child to talk. Question gently and make sure that your child knows that you are supportive. Do not push your child to give you information, but show that you are prepared to listen.

- Reporting the incident. In deciding whether to report the incident to the authorities, the adult must take into account the age of the child, the seriousness of the offence and what effect the ensuing court case may have on the child. Find out if videotaping is allowed instead of a court appearance being required. The adult also must consider the danger to other children if the offender is allowed to go free. If the abuse is reported, explain to the child that a policeman or woman, or another professional person would like to talk with him or her, and that the person's job is to help protect children. Stay with the child during the interview. You should also:

- Praise your child for having survived the attack. Explain that he or she had no choice at the time of the offence. Say that you are glad your child survived and that he or she is now safe. This often helps a child to come to terms with the question, 'What did I do wrong?' Later you can talk about how to keep safe in the future and teach preventative skills.

- Seek medical attention, if necessary. Explain to your child what the doctor will do and why. Make sure that the doctor is compassionate. Privately ask the doctor to reassure your child that his or her body is all right, despite the incident. Stay with your child during the examination.
- Seek help. Professional counselling or self-help groups may help to lessen the traumatic effect of the incident.
- Keep the structure of home. As much as possible, try not to change the routine of home or school. During times of stress this is helpful because it provides a structure to work within and should facilitate the healing process. If the offender is a family member, it must be decided what is in the best interests of the child.
- Reiterate that it is the offender's fault. Never tell your child that what happened was naughty or dirty. If you do, the child will assume that he or she is somehow to blame. Say the offender was naughty or wrong. For young children, you may want to liken it to a burglar taking something he or she had no right to take.
- Use puppets or dolls. With young children you may want to use toys to help them to discuss their feelings. This can also be helpful in teaching them some of the preventative techniques mentioned earlier.

Where to get help

The decision about getting outside help must be made according to the circumstances. Parents or other interested adults can contact either the local social services, a GP or the police. (Please note that if local authorities receive information suggesting that there are grounds for bringing care proceedings in respect of a child or young person, they have a statutory duty to investigate the case unless they consider it unnecessary.) In addition, there are several organisations listed below that offer help and advice. If you want to know the policy of the help organisation about reporting, ask before you proceed.

Family Network, c/o National Children's Home, 85 Highbury Park, London N5 1UD.
Scotland: dial 100 and ask for Freefone Family Network; north of England: (061) 236 9873; south of England: (0582) 422751.
Provides help for children and families with problems. There is a telephone counselling service.

Incest Crisis Line. Richard: (01) 422 5100, Shirley: (01) 890 4732, Anne: (01) 302 0570. 24-hour service.
A support group for anyone involved in an incestuous relationship, either past or present.

In Support of Sexually Abused Children. Susan Carr, PO Box 526, London NW6 1SU, tel. (01) 435 2973.
Offers support for sexually abused children and their parents.

Mothers of Abused Children. Chris Strickland, tel. (0965) 31432, Cumbria.
Support offered for mothers of sexually abused children.

National Society for the Prevention of Cruelty to Children.
Head Office, 64-74 Saffron Hill, London EC1N 8RS;
tel. (01) 242 1626. The Society operates in England, Wales and Northern Ireland. See directory for local branches.
The NSPCC aims to prevent child abuse in all forms and to give practical help to families with children at risk.

Organisation for Parents Under Stress (OPUS), 26 Manor Drive, Pickering, West Yorkshire WF5 0LL.
OPUS has a network of 30 self-help groups for parents under stress to prevent child abuse and maltreatment of infants and young children.

Parents Anonymous, 6 Manor Gardens, London N7 6LA; tel. (01) 263 8918, 6 pm to 6 am.
Parents Anonymous offers help to parents who are tempted to abuse their children and to those who have already done so. There are meetings and a telephone counselling and visiting service for parents by trained volunteer parents.

Rape Crisis Centres. For information on local branches telephone (01) 837 1600 or write to PO Box 42, London N6 9RJ.

Royal Scottish Society for the Prevention of Cruelty to Children, Melville House, 41 Polwarth Terrace, Edinburgh EH11 1NU; tel. (031) 337 8539/8530.

Samaritans. See directory for local numbers.
Samaritans are trained volunteers who talk with people about problems of depression and suicide.

Woman's Therapy Centre, 6 Manor Gardens, London N7 6LA; tel. (01) 263 6200.
Send a large SAE for list of groups and activities.

Do preventative techniques work?

The positive message of this book is that parents and adults who care about children do have ways of teaching children to stay safe. Despite the disturbing facts of child sexual assault, there is growing evidence of the effectiveness of preventative programmes like CAP. The following are only five of many reported incidents of children learning to keep themselves safe after they have been taught basic preventative techniques.

One 9-year-old girl was in a community centre toilet when a stranger tried to grab her. She responded with a loud yell and kicked him hard on the shin. This startled him long enough for her to run out and get help. The man fled with staff in pursuit, but got away. The child was safe.

After a CAP workshop, a 7-year-old boy revealed that a neighbour had touched him in his private parts the previous week. The child had been told that this was a 'special secret' not to be told to anyone. The parents were contacted, the family given supportive help and the offender was arrested. The child was saved from further molestation and seems to be recovering because of the way in which the situation was handled. He was believed, told that it was not his fault and praised for telling.

Twelve-year-old Jane and her 9-year-old brother, Edward, were walking through a large common area, when two teenage boys tried to attack Jane. Both children started shouting for help, kicked the attackers and made a general commotion. The teenagers ran away and the children went for help, contacting their parents who telephoned the police. The children were both shaken, but unhurt.

Three weeks after a CAP workshop, an 8-year-old girl told her teacher that her 15-year-old brother was coming into the bathroom while she was bathing and trying to touch her. The girl told him to leave her alone and with the help of the teacher told her mother. The abuse was stopped before it started and the boy received counselling.

A 14-year-old girl told her mother that her stepfather was coming into her bedroom at night and trying to kiss and fondle her. Although at first the mother did not believe her, the school social worker helped the mother to understand that the girl was telling the truth. The family received help from the social services.

By educating children about practical preventative techniques such as saying no, getting help and not keeping bad secrets, we are permitting them to use their judgement to protect themselves. By making sure that adults believe and help children, we can begin to combat effectively the problem of child sexual assault.

Appendix 1
Questionnaire on sexual assault for young teenagers

Questions

1. You have the right to be safe.	**T**	**F**
2. You should always keep secrets if you promise not to tell.	**T**	**F**
3. A bribe is given to make you do something you do not want to do.	**T**	**F**
4. People are either good or bad.	**T**	**F**
5. Only bad people who look strange hurt children.	**T**	**F**
6. Adults do not always believe children.	**T**	**F**
7. Children should always obey adults.	**T**	**F**
8. You sometimes have the right to break rules.	**T**	**F**
9. It is a good idea to answer the telephone by repeating your name or your telephone number.	**T**	**F**
10. You should never lie.	**T**	**F**
11. You should never fight back if someone attacks you.	**T**	**F**
12. You have the right to tell anyone, even someone you know and trust, not to touch you in any way which makes you feel uncomfortable.	**T**	**F**
13. Jealousy is a sign of true love.	**T**	**F**
14. You should never hurt anyone's feelings.	**T**	**F**
15. Looking foolish in front of others is really embarrassing.	**T**	**F**
16. Boys are usually encouraged to be sensitive and gentle with girls.	**T**	**F**
17. When a child is assaulted, the offender is usually a stranger.	**T**	**F**
18. Girls are assaulted much more often than boys.	**T**	**F**
19. The vast majority of attackers are men.	**T**	**F**
20. The best way to escape a potential assault is to vomit.	**T**	**F**
21. A 'real man' shows the girl that he is the boss.	**T**	**F**
22. Generally the more attractive a girl is the greater her chance of being assaulted.	**T**	**F**

Preventing Child Sexual Assault, © Michele Elliott 1985

23. It is sometimes the victim's fault that he/she was
assaulted.   **T   F**

24. People are much safer from assault at home.   **T   F**

25. If you or someone you know is assaulted, you should tell a
trusted adult immediately.   **T   F**

Answers

1. You have the right to be safe.　　　　　　　　　　**True**

2. You should always keep secrets if you promise not to
tell.　　　　　　　　　　　　　　　　　　　　　　**False**
**Some secrets should not be kept. If anyone asks
you to keep touching a secret or if you feel
confused, uncomfortable or frightened by a secret,
find a trusted adult to tell.**

3. A bribe is given to make you do something you do not
want to do.　　　　　　　　　　　　　　　　　　**True**

4. People are either good or bad.　　　　　　　　　　**False**

5. Only bad people who look strange hurt children.　　**False**

6. Adults do not always believe children.　　　　　　**True**
**If the first person you tell a problem to does not
believe you, keep telling until someone helps you.**

7. Children should always obey adults.　　　　　　　**False**
**In order to keep safe, it may be necessary to
disobey an adult.**

8. You sometimes have the right to break rules.　　　**True**
To keep safe, you have the right to break any rules.

9. It is a good idea to answer the telephone by repeating
your name or your telephone number.　　　　　　**False**

10. You should never lie.　　　　　　　　　　　　　**False**
**You might have to lie to keep safe. For example,
you could say that your mum was waiting for you
across the road if someone was bothering you.**

11. You should never fight back if someone attacks you.　**False**
**If you feel in danger, you should do whatever you
can to keep safe, such as kick, yell, bite, etc.**

12. You have the right to tell anyone, even someone you
know and trust, not to touch you in any way which

Preventing Child Sexual Assault, © Michele Elliott 1985

makes you feel uncomfortable.   **True**
You have the right to say who touches your body.

13. Jealousy is a sign of true love.   **False**
**Love depends upon mutual trust. Jealousy is
based upon lack of trust.**

14. You should never hurt anyone's feelings.   **False**
**In order to keep yourself safe, you may have to say
no to someone you know and like, which might
hurt his or her feelings.**

15. Looking foolish in front of others is really
embarrassing.   **True**
**But do not be afraid to look foolish if you feel
inside that something is wrong. If you think you
should leave a party, for example, because you do
not like what is happening, do leave even if you are
embarrassed. It might keep you safe.**

16. Boys are usually encouraged to be sensitive and gentle
with girls.   **False**
**Girls should make it clear to boys that they like
boys who are not afraid to be kind. Boys often
think that girls only like the 'macho' type.**

17. When a child is assaulted, the offender is usually a
stranger.   **False**
**Over 75 per cent of people who assault children are
known to the children.**

18. Girls are assaulted much more often than boys.   **False**
**Boys are almost as much at risk as girls, though
boys less often report an assault.**

19. The vast majority of assaults are committed by men.   **True**
**Over 90 per cent of reported assaults are
committed by men. However, most men would
never attack anyone.**

20. The best way to escape a potential assault is to vomit. **False**
**While it may work, conversations with offenders
indicate that these kinds of tactics make them
angry, rather than disgusted. Many people feel
that an immediate spirited physical self-defence,
including loud yelling, kicking, hitting, etc., is best
because the element of surprise helps the victim to
get away. Some people have successfully talked
their way out of dangerous situations. Each person
must decide what is best according to the
circumstances.**

21. A 'real man' shows the girl that he is the boss. **False**
Why should one partner be boss?

22. Generally the more attractive a girl is the greater her
chance of being assaulted. **False**
**Studies have shown that being physically
attractive has nothing to do with assault.**

23. It is sometimes the victim's fault that he/she was
assaulted. **False**
**It is always the offender's fault. No one deserves to
be assaulted.**

24. People are much safer from assault at home. **False**
**In a recent London survey, 51 per cent of assaults
happened either in the victim's or the assailant's
home.**

25. If you or someone you know is assaulted, you should tell
a trusted adult immediately. **True**
**Think about people who would believe you and
who would help you make a decision about what to
do. An assault is too big a burden to carry in secret
and getting help early will often lessen the trauma.**

Preventing Child Sexual Assault, © Michele Elliott 1985

Appendix 2
Questionnaire on sexual assault for older teenagers

Questions

1. You have the right to tell anyone, even someone you know and trust, not to touch you in any way which makes you feel uncomfortable. **T F**
2. When a girl says 'no' to a boy, she frequently means 'yes'. **T F**
3. A boy has a right to expect more than a kiss after he has spent money on a date. **T F**
4. Jealousy is a sign of true love. **T F**
5. Birth control is the female's responsibility. **T F**
6. Boys are not encouraged to be sensitive and gentle with girls. **T F**
7. Sexual frustration can be physically harmful. **T F**
8. Girls who fantasise about being seduced have emotional problems. **T F**
9. Most date rapes occur because a girl teases to the point that a boy cannot control himself. **T F**
10. Alcohol and/or drugs can lower inhibitions about engaging in sexual activity. **T F**
11. When a child is molested, the molester is usually a stranger. **T F**
12. Girls are molested much more often than boys. **T F**
13. The vast majority of sexual abusers are men. **T F**
14. The best way to escape a potential rapist is to vomit. **T F**
15. A 'real man' shows the girl that he is the boss. **T F**
16. Generally the more attractive a girl is the higher her chance of being sexually assaulted. **T F**
17. When a girl is sexually assaulted, she usually has done something to provoke it. **T F**
18. It is against the law for a boy to engage in sexual intercourse with a girl under 16, even with her consent. **T F**

Preventing Child Sexual Assault, © Michele Elliott 1985

19. Sexual gratification is the major reason for rape.   **T   F**

20. Males who are sexually assaulted suffer the same kind of emotional trauma as female victims.   **T   F**

21. People are much safer from sexual assault at home.   **T   F**

22. An assailant rarely finds it necessary to use a weapon to commit sexual assault.   **T   F**

23. Less than half of all rapes are reported to police.   **T   F**

24. People who sexually assault others are psychologically disturbed.   **T   F**

25. Rapists are secret, solitary offenders who usually attack their victims when the rapist is alone.   **T   F**

26. Teenage and adult victims of sexual assault seldom know the identity of the offender.   **T   F**

27. Sexual assault is usually an unplanned, spontaneous act.   **T   F**

28. There are many false reports of rape by women seeking revenge on their boyfriends.   **T   F**

29. If the victim feels uncomfortable talking with a male police officer, she has the right to request that a female officer be called.   **T   F**

30. Since the rape victim is often unprotected by contraceptives, she will probably become pregnant.   **T   F**

31. The victim is allowed to have a friend stay with her during the medical examination or questioning.   **T   F**

32. During an investigation of a rape, the victim can refuse to answer questions irrelevant to the rape.   **T   F**

33. If a woman is raped, her name will be published by the media reporting her case.   **T   F**

34. As a rule, the rape victim can be asked questions in court about her sexual conduct.   **T   F**

35. If you or someone you know has been sexually assaulted, you should tell a trusted adult immediately.   **T   F**

Answers

1. You have the right to tell anyone, even someone you
know and trust, not to touch you in any way which
makes you feel uncomfortable.   **True**
**Since a high percentage of the assaults on teenagers
are by an adult known to them, it is important to
learn to say no not only to strangers, but to friends,
family members or acquaintances.**

2. When a girl says 'no' to a boy, she frequently means
'yes'.   **False**
**This attitude is left over from old films and books.
Boys and girls should discuss together their ideas
about mixed messages so that both understand the
expectations and the misconceptions of the other.**

3. A boy has a right to expect more than a kiss after he has
spent money on a date.   **False**
If this is his attitude, 'go Dutch'.

4. Jealousy is a sign of true love.   **False**
**Love depends upon mutual trust. Jealousy is based
upon lack of trust.**

5. Birth control is the female's responsibility.   **False**
It should be a shared responsibility.

6. Boys are not encouraged to be sensitive and gentle with
girls.   **True**
**Most boys are raised to believe that being tough and
macho is what girls expect of them. This should be
discussed so that girls and boys can decide what
they value in a relationship.**

7. Sexual frustration can be physically harmful.   **False**
Boys have used this line for years!

8. Girls who fantasise about being seduced have emotional problems. **False**
Some girls have seduction fantasies. In the fantasy, they are in control; they choose the 'assailant', place, circumstances, etc. The reality of rape is different – violent and sadistic.

9. Most date rapes occur because a girl teases to the point that a boy cannot control himself. **False**
This attitude blames the victim. Rape occurs because the assailant has problems with anger, aggression, hostility and power.

10. Alcohol and/or drugs can lower inhibitions about engaging in sexual activity. **True**
Studies have shown this to be true for both sexes.

11. When a child is molested, the molester is usually a stranger. **False**
The child knows the attacker in at least 75 per cent of the reported cases of child molestation.

12. Girls are molested much more often than boys. **False**
Statistics vary, but boys are almost as much at risk as girls. The victimisation of boys is reported less often, partly because of the fear of being branded as a homosexual after an attack.

13. The vast majority of sexual abusers are men. **True**
Ninety per cent of reported attacks were committed by men.

14. The best way to escape a potential rapist is to vomit. **False**
While it may work, conversations with convicted rapists indicate that these kinds of tactics make them angry, rather than disgusted. Many people feel that an immediate spirited physical defence, including loud yelling, kicking, hitting, etc. is best

because the element of surprise would help the
victim to get away. Some people have successfully
talked their way out of rape, but each must decide
for herself according to the circumstances.

15. A 'real man' shows the girl that he is the boss.   **False**
**Why should one partner be the boss? This implies
that the girl is incapable of directing her own life. It
places her in the same category as a docile pet.**

16. Generally the more attractive a girl is the higher her
chance of being sexually assaulted.   **False**
**Studies of assault victims have shown that being
physically attractive has nothing to do with sexual
assault.**

17. When a girl is sexually assaulted, she usually has done
something to provoke it.   **False**
**In the United States, the National Commission on the
Causes and Prevention of Violence did a study on
crimes of violence and paid particular attention to
the role of the victim in cases of murder, assault,
robbery and rape. The commission wanted to
determine whether victims of these crimes in any
way provoked them or rashly touched off the action
against them. It was discovered that victims of rape
were responsible for less provocative behaviour or
unwitting collusion than victims of murder, assault
or robbery. The cases on file of the rape of
individuals of all ages, from 3-month-old babies to
97-year-old women, show how ridiculous this myth
really is.**

18. It is against the law for a boy to engage in sexual
intercourse with a girl under 16, even with her consent.   **True**
The legal age of consent is 16.

19. Sexual gratification is the major reason for rape. **False**
**Rape is about violence, not sex. If you hit someone
over the head with your rolling pin, it is not called
cooking.**

20. Males who are sexually assaulted suffer the same kind
of emotional trauma as female victims. **True**
**Sexual assault on males is reported even less often
than assault on females and there is no support
system, such as Rape Crisis Centres, for male
victims.**

21. People are much safer from sexual assault at home. **False**
**In a recent London survey, 51 per cent of sexual
assaults happened either in the victim's or the
assailant's home.**

22. An assailant rarely finds it necessary to use a weapon to
commit sexual assault. **True**
**Only a small proportion of sexual assaults involve
weapons. Most assailants use superior size and fear
to subdue victims.**

23. Less than half of all rapes are reported to police. **True**
Only one in twelve are reported.

24. People who sexually assault others are psychologically
disturbed. **False**
Most test as 'normal' on psychological tests.

25. Rapists are secret, solitary offenders who usually attack
their victims when the rapist is alone. **True**
**In only one in a hundred cases in the London survey
was there more than one assailant.**

26. Teenage and adult victims of sexual assault seldom
know the identity of the offender. **False**
**Over 60 per cent of attackers in the London survey
were known to the victim.**

27. Sexual assault is usually an unplanned, spontaneous act.   **False**
Most sexual assaults are planned.

28. There are many false reports of rape by women seeking revenge on their boyfriends.   **False**
In a study in New York of all the reported rapes in one year, only 2 per cent turned out to be false.

29. If the victim feels uncomfortable talking with a male police officer, she has the right to request that a female officer be called.   **True**
While a victim has the right to request this, the police have no obligation to provide a female officer. The police do try to comply with this request, if at all possible.

30. Since the rape victim is often unprotected by contraceptives, she will probably become pregnant.   **False**
Only a small percentage of rape victims become pregnant.

31. The victim is allowed to have a friend stay with her during the medical examination or questioning.   **True**
This can be a family member or close friend.

32. During an investigation of a rape, the victim can refuse to answer questions irrelevant to the rape.   **True**
Questions about a victim's personal life, not relevant to the rape, need not be answered.

33. If a woman is raped, her name will be published by the media reporting her case.   **False**
Rape victims are entitled to anonymity before, during and after the trial.

34. As a rule, the rape victim can be asked questions in court about her sexual conduct.   **False**

In court a rape victim may not be asked questions about her previous sexual conduct unless the judge is satisfied that these questions are relevant to the defence.

35. If you or someone you know has been sexually assaulted, you should tell a trusted adult immediately.   **True** Think about the people who would believe you and who would help you in making a decision about what to do. Sexual assault is too big a burden to carry in secret and getting supportive help early will often lessen the trauma. If you feel completely alone, telephone the local Rape Crisis Centre (the number is in the directory) or telephone the London office on (01) 837 1600 for information. If the offender is an adult who is known to the child or a family member, contact the Incest Crisis line on (01) 890 4732 or (01) 422 5100.

Sources of Further Information

BRITISH ASSOCIATION FOR THE STUDY AND PREVENTION OF CHILD ABUSE AND NEGLECT. 'Child Sexual Abuse', guidelines for social services departments, BASCAN, 1981.

COOPER, S., LUTLER, Y. AND PHELPS, C. *Strategies for Free Children: A leader's guide to child assault prevention*, Child Assault Prevention Project of Women Against Rape, Columbus, Ohio, 1984.

HALL, R. E. *Ask Any Woman: A London inquiry into rape and sexual assault*, Falling Wall Press, 1985.

KEMPE, R. S. AND KEMPE, C. H. *Child Abuse*, Fontana/Open Books, 1978.

MRAZEK, P. B., LYNCH, M. AND BENTOVIM, A. 'Recognition of Child Sexual Abuse in the United Kingdom' in Mrazek, P. B. and Kempe, C. H. (eds). *Sexually Abused Children and their Families*, Pergamon Press, 1981.

NATIONAL SOCIETY FOR THE PREVENTION OF CRUELTY TO CHILDREN. *Developing a Child Centred Response to Sexual Abuse*, NSPCC, 1984.

PORTER, R. (ed). *Child Sexual Abuse within the Family*, Tavistock Publications, 1984.

WEST, D. *Sexual Victimisation*, Gower Publishing Co. Ltd, 1985.